C*Bedside* HAT

A Book of Meditation & Inspiration

This is a Bedside Chat

Come and
Chat With Me...

Managing a Spiritual Life

- Gerry J. Tucker

SpiritWorks
P.O. Box 16311
Austin, Texas 78761
www.TheSpiritWorks.net

Ordering information: Quantity sales. Special discounts are available on quantity purchases by corporations, associations, and others. For details, contact the publisher at the address above. Orders on-line with various trade bookstores and wholesalers such as Amazon: www.amazon.com.

IFX Publishing, Lago Vista, Texas
Printed in the United States of America

Bedside Chat: A Book of Meditation and Inspiration by Gerry J. Tucker
ISBN10: 0-9909790-4-0
ISBN13: 978-0-9909790-4-3

Non-fiction: Inspirational, Motivational, Self-Help and Spiritual. First Edition
This book is not a substitute for the medical advice of a physician or therapist. The reader should regularly consult a physician in matters relating to his/her health and particularly with respect to any symptoms that may require diagnosis or medical attention. Although the author and publisher have made every effort to ensure that the information in this book was correct at press time, the author and publisher do not assume and hereby disclaim any liability to any party. The intent of the author is only to offer information of a general nature to help you in your quest for spiritual fitness. In the event you use any of the information in this book for yourself, which is your constitutional right, the author and the publisher assume no responsibility for your actions.

Book Design by W. Muse Greenwood, Inspiration FX, IFX Publishing
Cover Design by Alan Greenwood
www.ifxpublishing.com
Author's Photograph by Korey Howell Photography

ACKNOWLEDGEMENTS

Thanks be to God for giving me a life of purpose, love, opportunity and grace. As a young girl I was inspired and molded by my experience at New Hope Baptist Church, Newark, New Jersey. It gave me the foundation of belief in God, faith, and trusting and without it I would not have been able to create this book.

Thanks to my Muse, W. Muse Greenwood who made *Bedside Chat* a reality. It would not have been possible without her guidance, direction and encouragement. A task master and spiritual writer, Muse believed in this project and made it happen. Thanks for taking care of my baby.

Thanks to Alan Greenwood for his quiet intervention to ensure all things went well.

A writer needs a friend who will be honest and helpful. Thanks to Ed Paulson for encouraging me, listening, and providing me open feedback to make this book about the reader.

Thanks to Joseph Measel for reviewing the early draft and editing it.

Thanks to Dr. Barbara Mink and Steve Camkin for the wonderful nature pictures from Utah.

Thanks to Carmen Tucker and Almaree Owens for their belief in me and encouragement. Thanks to Sharrion Jenkins and Mary Chance for their work on getting the website up and running in time for production.

To the many friends and family that supported the *Beside Chat* newsletters over the years, it's finally in your hands.

May God continue to bless all of you.

CONTENTS

Introduction

For several years I had the pleasure of writing Bedside Chat, a spiritual newsletter for one hundred of my favorite friends. The newsletter focused on spiritual principles, biblical quotes, and words of inspiration. I started the newsletter at a point in my life when I needed to reflect on spiritual principles and begin to use them. I needed a way to make spiritual principles real and confirm that they worked for me. So, I created a newsletter in which I would share with my readers those spiritual principles which I wanted to integrate into my life, the biblical quotes I relied upon, and I described my experiences with actualizing the principles. Some experiences were more successful than others. What I learned from writing the newsletter was that it's easier to write about them rather than integrate them. Writing about the principles did reinforce what I needed to do differently to have a successful life. I also needed to meditate on the spiritual principles to better understand the process of how to use them in my life. This book represents the meditations that were developed to reinforce the spiritual principles. Thus, I have used the newsletters as the foundation for this book.

The meditations and inspirational essays in this book are meant to guide you in how to address the challenging issues in life and live a spiritual life. Life is full of opportunities and challenges, none of which we get to choose. Every day brings opportunities to learn something new if we will open ourselves to what is happening around us and make a conscious choice to grow emotionally, physically, and spiritually. The best we can do is learn from our experiences, learn from the experiences of others, and integrate what we learn into our life. The meditations and essays are designed to provide a framework for looking at and understanding those challenging issues, what to expect in transition, how to manage it, how to get the energy to move on with life when you have lingered too long, and how to hold onto your truth and faith in challenging times.

The challenge of living a spiritual life is maintaining faith and trust in God, no matter what is happening in life or in the lives of our love ones. We can espouse spiritual principles, but if we don't hold onto them when we are challenged our journey is a struggle. If we struggle we don't get to experience the grace, joy, and peace that God promises us. When we encounter difficult times, we need to meditate and pray on the word of God and "know that you know" God is real and right there in the midst of everything.

Over the years, I have gotten wisdom and inspiration from reading books. Reading helps me feel centered and it gives me insight in the midst of chaos. It is my desire that this book will provide the same space for you. It is only when we create the space to be still and reflect, can we see the truth of what's really happening in our lives and make good decisions. Transition, change, and loss are a consistent theme in life and it is my desire that you will read something in this book that will give you a way to look at your challenges and opportunities and give you peace. I hope the spiritual principles you need to integrate in your life are reinforced and, by reading this book, you will be assured there is a greater force in the universe to assist you in achieving your goals and purpose. I hope this book will help you get in touch with that universal spirit that can guide you to a spiritual life of peace, joy, and happiness.

How to Use This Book

When you're ready to retire for the evening, I hope you will reach for Bedside Chat as a way to unwind from the challenges of the day as you relax. Think about what's foremost in your mind and concentrate on that concern. Then, locate a topic or title in Bedside Chat that speaks to your heart or concern. Some of the poems and essays have activities. You will benefit by completing the activities and reflecting on your responses to them. If you don't feel like writing, feel free to draw pictures.

There is a "Let's Chat" section at the end of each chapter to help you reflect on how to better manage your situation. This is meant to be your journal. If you already have a journal, keep it close by your bedside and make notes in it after your nightly readings of Bedside Chat.

You are not expected to read this book in one sitting. Depending upon your mood and concerns, you may or may not choose to read a complete chapter. Skip around as the spirit leads you. If you have difficulty choosing a selection, just close your eyes, reflect on your concerns, and randomly open the book. Ask the spirit to guide you to an answer. An answer may come in many forms and Bedside Chat is just one of them.

It is important to read this book when you are at rest and in a space that supports your spiritual development. You will need to be in a quiet space, alone, and focused on a goal – creating the space to spiritually grow. You can only grow in spirit when you are free to explore your internal feelings and thoughts and tap into the God spirit that guides you. Read a little each night until you can read a passage and know that you have mastered that skill or task or learned the lesson. Read until you find a message meant just for you. Your heart will tell you when it's time to move on. May you sleep in peace.

Dedication

This book is dedicated to my Mom who wrote many stories and poems in her mind and heart. I found some of them upon her death and it was then that I came to know the extent of her love for poetry and writing. I knew she loved to read and she often wrote before retiring for the evening. I now know the joy she felt in retreating to the spirit within.

Also, to my loving daughter, Carmen, who taught me unconditional love and gave more than she received. I am so proud of the woman she has become. Her support of me and my journey is overwhelming. One day soon, I look forward to reading her book.

This book is in celebration of my friendship with Dot, who would if she could, but she can't. So, I wrote this book with her in my mind and heart.

To my brother, George Jenkins Sr., and my sister, Joyce Ford, who kept up with me wherever I travelled and sent me their love and prayers. We have shared this journey together and I wouldn't want it any other way.

To my sisters who, over the years, supported and loved me, even when I didn't deserve it. Thank you my friends - Almaree Owens, Sharrion Jenkins, Delores ("Gino") Brown, Rhonda Fenner, Rosa Hunt, Dr. Barbara Mink, Sandy Hayden, Dr. Dot Tucker, Roxann Chargois, Marjon Christopher, Susan Johnson, Dr. Carla Emery-Culberson and Darlene Fields-Harris. Thanks for believing in me and reading the Bedside Chat newsletters from the begining.

To my other friends and family too numerous to list but, so loving and supportive, I thank you for encouraging and believing in me.

May God continue to bless all of you.

Chapter One

Peace, Hope,

Life is full of challenges whether at home, in the workplace, with friends or family. Challenges encourage us to grow and develop. As we manage these challenges

and Love

we learn to resolve life and work issues. Often when challenges are not resolved, they continue to show up in a variety of ways until the issue gets addressed ("Life's Beach Ball"). It is during these times we can find peace ("Finding Peace") in knowing there is perfect timing for all things ("God's Perfect Timing"). We must know there is a light at the end of the tunnel and we must recognize that "God is in Everything." In meeting your challenges I wish you a life of peace, hope, and love.

Peace can be found

In the stillness,

In love,

In knowing that God loves you

and only wants the best for you...

Write the vision...

"Then the Lord answered me and said:
Write the vision, and make it plain on tablets,
that he may run who reads it.
For the vision is yet for an appointed time;
But at the end it will speak, and it will not lie:
though it tarries, wait for it;
because it will surely come,
it will not tarry."

Habakkuk 2:2-3

When one contemplates how to live a life that makes a difference, it can be like putting a puzzle together. You have all the pieces, you just need to know the sequence. It is much more difficult to create the puzzle when you have no picture or vision. God has not only the vision, pieces, and sequence, but also perfect timing.

If you took a clean sheet of paper and had to create a puzzle of your life, what would it look like? What pieces of your life would you put together? Would you create it from where you are or from where you want to be? Could you define the different parts? Would you center on where you are right now or dream a *Big* dream? Where you are right now may not be where you will be tomorrow. Who knows tomorrow? We certainly don't, even though we think we do.

God is working behind the scenes to accomplish things we cannot see. It is not intended that we understand what God is doing. Our job is to live boldly and enjoy life since tomorrow is not promised. Our job is to fully live for today. We can only live one day at a time and enjoy the present moment. God has a plan and purpose for our life and we must live our life in the sequence of God's perfect timing.

You may have to wait to see what God is doing in your life. You may be asking for an answer and it has not yet come. In God's timing, every problem or situation that you are praying about has an answer. Walk in the spirit every day knowing that God will answer you. Listen carefully and consider God's plan for your life. God's timing is perfect.

God's Perfect Timing

Finding Peace

I recently overheard a telephone conversation between two friends. It was apparent they were both angry. When they ended the conversation, I could feel tension in the air. I tried to talk with my friend about the argument, but she was too high strung to calm down and listen to reason.

It is often in those moments when we lose control that we should withdraw, seek inner peace, and pray. When you feel angry, frustrated, or in pain, don't lash out at others or play to win, simply withdraw into your heart. In that very moment, be still and invoke God's grace and peace.

We often feel the need to "have our say" or "set the record straight" and, even, "get in the last word." Consider the big picture, does it deserve that much energy? Should it take up that much space in your precious life? Too often we're invested in winning, hanging onto our position, only to end up losing the argument. What we really need is inner peace. Inner peace can be achieved when you know and feel that God is in control. You won't need to have the last word; God has already had the last word. With peace, you can say what needs to be said in a way that it will be received and you'll be able to gracefully walk away. When you have peace there's no winner or loser, only peaceful closure.

Peace within is assurance that God is working in your life. It is a feeling of calmness, not because of anything specific, but in spite of everything. Throughout the day, when you find yourself getting upset or feeling out of sorts, slow down, examine your heart, and know that God is right there where you are and you can tap into inner peace.

OUR CHAT...

What are you wrestling with in your life?

How do you usually respond to stressful moments or situations?

What can you do differently to achieve peace for yourself?

Life's Beach Ball

I watched as a woman put a beach ball under water in the pool. She was trying to submerge it so the ball would stay underwater. However, it kept popping up and she kept trying to put it underwater. Frustrated, she gave up and let the beach ball float on the water.

What is the beach ball in your life? What's that thing that keeps showing up to let you know it's still there no matter how much you try to push it under. Whatever it is, face it today. It may be a person, situation, unresolved conflict, a lesson not yet learned, or something you've put off doing. Whatever it is, bring it to the surface and resolve it. It is important to achieve closure in our communications and relationships so that you can move on in peace. In order to get closure you must get quiet, don't analyze what's going on, just bring it to mind and let your thoughts flow. In acknowledging where you are, you'll be able to find solutions to your concerns.

Take your beach ball to God. Hold it up to Him and ask God to take it out of the water and assist you in seeing it clearly as well as showing you what you need to do differently. Once you can see clearly, you'll be able to let things flow. After all, God says, "Therefore I say unto you, take no thought for your life, what ye shall eat; neither for the body, what ye shall put on. Life is more than meat, and the body is more than raiment. Consider the ravens, for they neither sow nor reap, which have neither storehouse nor barn; and God feedeth them. How much more are ye better than the fowls?" (Luke 12:22-24).

OUR CHAT...

The beach ball in my life is:

I plan to let it go by doing these things:

Affirmation:
I let it go. I give it to God.

Cast your fate to the wind. Believe that if you persist in believing,

it must soon come true. For what is life, but having hope in our beliefs?

Living a Life of Truth

Our lives speak not only through what we say and do
but, more importantly by what we would never say or do.
You say, "I love you and I could never do or say anything to hurt you."
But, you do.
When you do, that's your true self showing up.
When life is truly about not hurting others
in words or deeds,
then, you can truly love, and your life will speak its truth.
When life is about giving, more than you receive,
then, you will be living a life of truth.

A Light at the End of the Tunnel

I see the light at the end of the tunnel;
Each day, I try to get closer to the truth,
I try hard to understand its secret,
To touch its sides and feel its roots.
Some days the light gets brighter;
Some days, it seems quite dim,

But I know by the end of springtime,
This old tunnel will give in.
Then I'll see the light of day,
A new sun bursting forth,
Then I'll know the path, my way;
The dawn of a bright and happy day.

God Is In Everything

I don't remember when I first found God. I remember enjoying Sunday School, the church choir, dinner at church after service, and the sermons (which I didn't understand at the time). I felt loved and part of a greater, spiritual family. I did not relish leaving church on Sunday since our minister was a wonderful teacher. His messages touched my soul and made me feel worthy of God's love.

In the early days I thought God was in Heaven and Satan was in hell. I later came to realize God is in everything. He's in the air, wind, food, water, trees, birds, and man. God is spirit moving in and through us. When we learn to tap into our spirit, we can feel the love of God.

Last night, I sat on the porch and watched the trees dance in the wind. It was like a melodious symphony with crescendos and cymbals playing God's music, letting me know that God was right there where I was sitting. I was mesmerized by the trees swaying in the breeze. I tried to see the wind as it moved through the branches. I could only see the trees easily swaying. God is somewhat like the wind in the trees. You can't see Him but, you can feel His presence. When you sit in the quiet of night and get still, you can feel God's presence in your soul. When everything else is quiet, you can feel the warmth of God's touch. God is in everything.

OUR CHAT...

When do you feel closest to God?

How do you tap into your spirit?

Has God spoken to your spirit? How did you know it was God?

God Is Faithful

Sometimes in the midst of a crisis, you might ask, "Where is God?" or "Why does God let these things happen to me?" We don't know the answer. We do know that life is about growth, experiences, and lessons learned. God didn't promise there wouldn't be storms. God did promise to be with us through the storm.

Each time you encounter a negative experience, you should look for the positive and ask, "What is the lesson to be learned?" or "What is the good that can come from this situation?" Sometimes, it is impossible to see the good at the time however, you must know and believe that God has a plan for your life, and you will endure the cycles.

There are cycles throughout life. There will be times of sadness and times of joy. No one is exempt from life's challenges. It is your job to be strong, through faith, knowing that God is always in control. You must know that you are worthy of receiving an answer from God. Think about the miracles of life. Don't you feel the wind, even though you can't see it? Can you see God in the flowers that were once little seeds? Do you see God in the sunrise and sunset? Who, but God, could create such a sight? You, too, are God's creation. God is faithful. He is right there where you are; you do not need to beg or demand that God appear. If you sit quietly and pray in peaceful surroundings, God will hear you.

Challenges are meant to draw you closer to God. God knows what you need. Don't feel that you must do something extraordinary to get God's attention. If you have the faith of a mustard seed, God will answer your prayer. God only wants the best for you. When challenges show up in your life, rather than react, get quiet and tap into your heart. Hold the challenge firmly in your hands and hand it off to God on a silver platter. Whether it's a broken heart, a job, a family situation, finances, or something you just can't handle, God will take it and fix it. Pray for peace. Pray for understanding. Pray for discernment. Pray for good health. Pray for others. Then, count your blessings and reflect on what God has done thus far in your life. God is faithful and God will answer your prayers.

God is our refuge and strength, an ever present help in trouble.
(Psalm 46:1).

OUR CHAT...

What is it you're praying about? Do you feel that God is listening? If not, what do you want God to know about your concerns?

Has there been a time in your life when you thought God wasn't listening, but you got an answer? What happened and what was the answer from God?

Believing in an unlimited God

The power of God is only limited by our conscious and unconscious beliefs. If we limit our beliefs to what we know is possible then, we are restricting God to our boundaries, parameters and perceptions. To perceive an unlimited God we have to set aside what we know to be true and remember God's promises to his people. God promises to deliver more than we could ever imagine.

A Glad Heart

I watched the night turn to morning.
The night light was a backdrop for the mountains in the distance.
Rainbow colors filled the sky.
The mountains kissed the rainbow
and my heart was made glad.

The writing in the sky seemed to have a message I could not decipher.
I stared until there was an opening in the clouds,
I was hoping to get a glimpse of its meaning.
Morning burst through the clouds
announcing it's a brave new day
and my heart was made glad.

The sun rose to bless the morning,
The mountain's silhouette stood still as if to say, "I'm here."
The wind began to blow;
The birds began to sing;
The flowers and trees swayed.
And my heart was made glad.

A country road is much too long to walk the path of life, alone.

I need
God to
walk with
me.

LET'S CHAT...

What can you conclude about your life after reading
this chapter?

Do you feel you are at peace? Are you full of hope? Are
you in love with life?

If not, why not? What do you need to do to achieve peace
in your life?

What can you do differently?

Chapter Two

Change is inevitable and unavoidable in everyone's life. It might be the loss of a friend or family member, divorce ("Dance with Divorce"), a relationship you just can't let go of ("Give It Up"), loss of a job, or maybe it's just a time of chaos and uncertainty ("Life's Unfolding"). To manage change and get on the other side, we must realize that change is a process ("Transition is a Process") and it can't be rushed. It has a natural progression and often, if we can listen to our heart and spirit ("Waiting for an Answer"), be still ("Stillness") and mindful, and we will find the answer to every challenge ("Turn It Over").

In Transition

CHANGE...

Change is inevitable.
We fight it. We are fearful and frightened of it.
When in reality we must face it, feel it, and explore it.

We must walk through the stages of change and transition.
We can't go around it. We can't retreat from it.
When we walk through the stages and get on the
other side, we can look back in awe, release the past,
and live in expectation of a better future.
Go with the flow of change.

A Dance with Divorce

We took to the dance floor for a "swing" dance. It felt as if our bodies melted into one another. Around the room we whirled and I felt like I was on a cloud jammin' to the best music in the world. Our marriage was one dance after another. Finally, the music stopped.

Dancing can be difficult. You need to have the right partner, right music, and right timing. As you dance, you wonder whether you are in step with one another or dancing to a different tune. Are you going in the same direction or wanting to go your separate ways? Is it better to keep on dancing or dance to the music alone? When I realized my partner was dancing with another, I decided to dance with divorce.

No doubt, divorce is a painful event. No matter how much it is wanted by either party, it hurts. When children are involved, divorce can be even more complex, ugly, and emotional. To dance with divorce, you will need to be internally strong. At times, the pain may be unbearable because you can't imagine life without your partner who is no longer dancing with you.

Divorce represents an ending. There is no easy way to bring about an ending. Unlike other endings, the ending of a divorce is a process that continues even after the papers are signed. However, to end it you must walk through the hurt and pain and get on the other side. When you are ready for another relationship, the sun will shine again. You will again love and be loved. You will have a bright future.

As you walk through divorce, respect yourself and your values. You can't change who you are, but you can communicate to your partner what's important (values) in letting go, what you need (expectations) to have a secure future, and what is needed to mend the relationship. There will be differences because you're individuals. There should also be points on which you can agree; focus on the points of agreement. You should expect discord, but plan for harmony.

Remember, you are worthy. You are worthy of the attention, trust, emotion, and support that a marriage can provide. Don't settle for less. Be confident that if two individuals want a marriage to work and will work on it, it can be successful. The dance can be enjoyable.

God didn't promise there would always be sunshine. God promised to walk with you through the pain. When you're about to dance with divorce, walk with God.

Give up what no longer works for you.
Let it go.
Bury it in the dirt.
Give it to the wind.
Write it on a note and throw it away.
Take it from your heart and your spirit.
If it no longer works for you, you no longer need it.
Give up what no longer works for you.
Let it go, let it go, let it go.

Give It Up

What is it that no longer works for you?

What do you gain by holding on to it?

Are you ready to give it up? If not, why not?

What do you need to do to let go of it?

OUR CHAT...

I held on to it as long as I could. I have to *let it* go or *lose* my "self".

Riding the Rivers of Life

As the river flows to the sea, life also flows.
Sometimes the river flows quietly and peacefully.
At other times, it flows rapidly and dangerously.
As we learn to navigate the rivers of life, we must keep moving, striving to reach our destiny.

In life, there are times when we want to stop the flow and slow down and there will be other times when we're just trying to keep up.

Our challenge is to stay in the flow of life while finding ways to survive the ebb and flow.
At all times, we must remember — God is our source and supply.

We must look to God to calm the rivers and angry seas.
Ride the rivers of life with God.

To make this transition, I must shift from my ego — mental state, to my spiritual, God-like state. Totally and completely.

Life's Unfolding

Life unfolds one day at a time and each day we get to make choices. As life unfolds, it's important to minimize panic and reacting or overreacting to the day's activities or people. Our success is determined by how we manage the stress brought on by the day's events. We must learn to take one day at a time, to be present in each moment, and to make the best of that day.

Like the waves of the ocean, no matter how much you want to see the next wave, there is a cycle. The tide will flow one wave at a time, no sooner, no later. So, slow down your life. Enjoy each day for what it brings to you and be grateful for that day. Look for the challenge. Look for the opportunity to touch another person's life with kindness and goodness.

When you approach the day with curiosity and hope, God will show up. Look for God in everything and watch life unfold with grace.

Transition is a Process

Life brings one transition after another. Sometimes, it is expected and, at other times, it is unexpected. At some point in life, you will experience a life change over which you have no control. It may be an illness, death of a loved one, loss of a dream or job, or you may feel the need to go in another direction. These changes are the most challenging.

There is no one way or easy way to manage change. The stages of change may take a person through chaos, numbness, exploration, and exhilaration. It is during these times that you must remember, "I am a child of God." God is always there. God hears you and will take care of you.

As with any process, don't fight change. Learn to feel it, be still with it, and tap into your inner spirit. When it's time to move on and act, the spirit will guide you.

When you feel like you must make a decision, act or react, or just do something, that is the time to be still, meditate on God's words, and wait on God for direction. God is in control. God will manage the transition, if you let go. God is guiding you. Let life flow. May God bless you in your transition.

OUR CHAT...

Are you experiencing a life change?

How are you feeling in the meantime?

How do you want to feel when your transition is complete?

OUR CHAT...

Are you in a transition? Describe it.

Are you learning to live in the present moment? If not,
why not?

What are you hoping God will unfold in
your life?

What are you doing in the meantime while you wait for
God's direction?

There are many ways to describe the stages of life. You can define it by your experiences, by the people in your life, family events, or your age. Through all these stages, we are learning and growing into the person God would have us to be.

A friend recently conveyed to me that she was living at the intersection of "adventure" and "impulse." Describing life by intersections was new to me. I asked her to explain this concept. She said, "there are times when life is filled with adventure and other times when one totally acts on impulse." It was an accurate description of her. She loves to travel, thinks big, won't take no for an answer, and if she thinks of doing

something, it's done.

After our conversation, I considered how I would describe the intersections of my life. On the one hand, there is chaos, ambiguity, and stress - most of it self-induced. On the other hand, I experience a lot of love from family and friends, success and fun. I experience more fun and laughter than usual, aging does that to you. After careful examination I decided that I live at the intersection of "practicality" and "spirituality."

I chose practicality because, at this point in my life, it's important to be grounded, successful in what I choose to do, and financially secure. I don't make a move without considering the long term effects of a decision. I am neither as

The Intersections of Life

impulsive as my friend nor as I was in my earlier years. Being a practical problem solver, I always want to know who, what, and why. I don't always directly ask the question, but it's usually on my mind.

I chose spirituality since I have finally gotten to the point in life when I am able to let it go and give it to God. I remind myself and others that God is in control. This works well in the workplace when you have to let things take its course and try not to control people. The tendency is to want to "fix it" (and people), and make things right (meaning your view of what's right). I have learned to listen and let the process take its course. Spirituality has helped me to tap into my heart and listen to that small, quiet voice before

taking action. Taking time to explore my feelings and seek the spiritual approach let's me make better decisions.

Spirituality helps me take the high road and stay "above the line." It lets me know it's not about me. It's about being an instrument for good in the lives of others. When we act out of love and spirit, we are able to effectively resolve issues and mend relationships. I'm still on the spiritual road and I'm further along today than before. How about you?

How would you describe the intersections of your life? What descriptive terms would you use to define where you are in life? What crossroads are you facing? Are you comfortable with where you are or are you preparing for a change?

Let him who walks in the dark,
who has no light,
Trust in the name of the Lord
and rely on his God.
- Isaiah 50:10

Waiting for an Answer

A friend recently confided that she was depressed and heartbroken over her impending divorce, after thirty years of marriage. She felt alone and numb. She couldn't move forward. While her married women friends envied her new life, her family felt the heart wrenching pain and anguish of her loss. Even though I shared with her my own experiences with divorce, I could not console her.

At some point in life, each of us will have a catastrophic, unexpected, or devastating experience. No one is immune. It may not be a divorce, it may be cancer or other illness, loss of a child or family member, loss of a dream, loss of a job, or just plain depression. After all, life happens. It is during these times we must remember that we are God's children and, just as a mother cares for her children, God cares for us.

As with any transition, there will come a time when you simply need to be still and tap into your inner spirit for guidance. When you do, you will hear the voice of the spirit, just as plain as you can see the sky. God will touch your spirit and give you a message. God does not leave us. When it is time to move on, the inner spirit will let you know.

Often we're too busy to think it's just that easy. We feel we must make a decision or we must do something. When, in fact, you just need to go to God in prayer and wait for an answer. God hears you. God is right there with you. God will bless you wherever you are today.

$\mathcal{S}$ometimes in life when we don't know the answer, We just need to be still, step aside, and __

Let God work it out.

OUR CHAT...

What transition are you experiencing?

Are you able to be still?

What do you need to do to get through this transition?

What tool can you use to better manage the transition?

Stillness

The most difficult phase of transition is stillness. Stillness is when you must sit with the sadness, frustration, depression, anger, fear, or loss. It requires you to face the difficulty and actually feel the need for change. During stillness, you are working on accepting the reality that your life has or is about to change. Your emotions will fluctuate and you may experience "highs" and "lows" for no known reason. The key during this time of chaos is to just be still.

In stillness, you may feel numb or not responsive, but at the same time you will feel a sense of peace. You will know it is time to move on when you begin to explore your options and possibilities. You will minimize the feelings of hurt, anger, fear, or frustration and replace those feelings with optimism. When you learn to sit in stillness and not fight it, you will be able to move on. Moving on means you are ready to explore, plan, release the past, and define the future. It is a time of new beginnings, new values, and a new attitude. A life transition is a process and stillness is the bridge you must cross in order to get to the other side.

TURN IT OVER

Trusting in the Lord is the foundation of spirituality and religion. While we know that trusting is important, we are not always ready to tap into God's words, particularly in times of struggle and chaos, and trust Him. It is during these times that we feel we should be able to work things out. We are challenged to let go and give it to God.

To integrate trust into our everyday life, we need to use tangible strategies to truly "turn it over to God." Turning it over means you have to find what works for you, but whatever you do try to really, really trust God and let it go.

Some ways to turn it over include:

✓ Write the challenge or perplexing problem on a sheet of paper. Writing from the heart and voicing your concerns on paper somehow provides a feeling of release. When you have finished writing, fold it, tear it up, and throw it away. If you think about it again, remind yourself that you have given it to God.

✓ Put your prayer in a prayer box. The objective is to put it in the box and leave it there.

✓ Burn incense or light a candle. They are both a signal that help is needed, whether it's for you or someone else.

✓ Sit quietly and talk with God. God hears our every need, our every cry, and our every prayer.

✓ Fast, meditate, and pray.

If you truly believe God loves you, then know that God will answer your prayers. Turn it over to God.
-Genny J. Tucker

"Trust in the Lord
with all your heart,
lean not on your own
understanding."

Proverbs 3:5

How do you manage change in your life? Are you comfortable with change? What can you do differently to better manage change?

Chapter Three

Getting Unstuck

When faced with a challenge, there comes a time when a decision must be made. We can either stay stuck or move on. In Getting Unstuck, you will learn to accept that you don't get everything you want ("When God Won't Give Me What I Want") and, sometimes, we even need to put our "self" aside ("Step Aside") so God can work, especially in affairs of the heart. We know we can't change people, yet we try. Loss of love or a relationship means letting go of a little of oneself ("When Love Is Not Enough") and saying goodbye to a dream. However, if we hold onto our faith and trust in God, an Angel will appear and help us with a "New Beginning."

It is often difficult to
wait for God's will to show up
in our lives.
If we remain faithful,
All things work together
for our good.

When God Won't Give Me What I Want

A friend shared with me that she was not receiving good gifts from the universe. I inquired as to why she thought she was not receiving God's gifts. She simply said, "I guess God doesn't want me to have them."

Often, when we pray for something and it doesn't come, we want to believe God is withholding our good. Maybe we should focus on the answer as to why it doesn't come. It may be that it's not right for us, the timing is off, we're being selfish, or we're not being specific enough. We won't always know God's will for our life, but if we keep centered on God, knowing that all things work together for God's purposes, we can find peace.

Learn to accept that God is good, even during failures and heartbreaks. When you wait in frustration or sadness, you are not showing your faith in God. Ask for God's will to be done in your life and wait upon God with joy and expectation, knowing that God always cares about you and will give you what you need.

"Trust in the Lord, and do good. Delight in the Lord
And he shall give you the desires of your heart.
Commit your way to the Lord,
Trust also in Him,
and He shall bring it to pass.
He shall bring forth your righteousness as the light,
and your justice as the noonday.
Rest in the Lord, and wait patiently for him."

- Psalm 37:3-7

OUR CHAT...

Are you waiting for an answer from God?

Are you able to wait in peace and expectation?

What answer do you want?

Step Aside

There comes a time in one's life when you face a catastrophe that challenges your very being. You may find yourself in a situation that is unfathomable, unconscionable or something that you never imagined would happen to you. You ask God, "Why?" There is silence. No answer. No response. No stirring of the soul.

We have to remember that God works differently from man. Whereas we want things instantaneously, God designs things in big pictures. We only know yesterday. God knows yesterday, today and tomorrow. We anticipate in fear and anxiety. God plans in peace and grace.

When you don't know where to turn and friends can't soothe your troubled mind, turn within to God. Imagine that you are before God, thank God for the peace that God gives you and ask God to work a miracle in your life. God can give you peace like a river, calmness like the warm summer air, and joy like raindrops dancing on the ocean.

God is the only miracle worker. God is the only one that can change what seems impossible to man. God is a way maker. When you think you're at the end of the road, the sun will shine and you will see God working in your situation.

Life is a series of ups and downs. It's easy to be up when things are going well. It's in the midnight hour when you're alone and feeling the pain that you can go to God in prayer and ask in His name to change things. God always answers prayers. He never leaves us alone with our problems. He is in the midst of everything and promises that "all things work together for good to those that love the Lord." So, take your cares to God and know that God is in control. Lay your concerns at his feet and know that you will never walk alone. God loves you and God will work it out for you.

Step aside. Get your fears, your anxieties, and your hurts out of the way and let God work it out. God can do it ever so better than we could ever imagine. He can open doors that we haven't even dreamed about and more. You are God's child and God is right there with you. So, go gently into the night and cast your cares upon God. Joy comes tomorrow morning. Know that God is good. God wants only good for you. Step aside and let God do His thing.

Indian Summer

In the midst of Indian summer,
I could not change to accommodate the seasons.
I could not see beyond the sunlight of day or the
warmth of night.

I knew the time had come to move forward and
leave the past behind.
I knew it was time to grow and expand.
I knew today would be tomorrow's yesterday and
time would not stand still.

How could I tell you the sun no longer rose or
set by your smile?
How could I tell you that I was glad you were
gone?
How could I say the bells no longer rang when I
was in your arms?
I knew that we had grown apart.
Like two separate branches on the same tree, each
reaching toward the sky trying to reach higher
heights.
With all of this, I knew not how to say *"good-bye."*

*In the midst of Indian Summer, I could not change to
accommodate the seasons of my life.*

OUR CHAT...

Do you need to get unstuck from a person or situation?

What is holding you back?

What do you need to do to be happy and at peace??

Licking
My Wounds Still

There are golden moments in our lives that we recall over and over again. There are memorable times and some not so memorable times. Some moments are joyful; others are remorseful. Sometimes, there are exciting times, and then, there are challenging times. Moments in life are memories that are forever deeply ingrained in our hearts and minds. We get to choose which memories to hold onto and which memories to let go.

In my house, we treasured moments, but there were also genuine "sayings" in response to those moments that were passed down from generation to generation. Upon telling my mother of unfair treatment by my brothers, my mother would say, "What goes around comes around." I never understood what she meant, but as the years progressed I not only understood, but I became my mother. She would also say, "You'll never miss your water until your well runs dry," or "When life gives you lemons, make lemonade." I'm sure you have heard these sayings and have some of your own.

These sayings help us decide how we're going to handle life's challenges. With each challenge we get to make a life choice. We get to decide what's important to us. We get to choose how we respond to a situation, positively or negatively. Our choice determines whether we harbor resentment or are able to move forward.

If we continue to harbor resentment or maintain a negative attitude about life, we will feel wounded and stuck. Wounds take a long time to heal. So, if you're still licking your wounds from the past, know that "this, too, will pass." Don't hold onto anger, frustration, or hate. Life is too short and you could have been dealt a different hand. Heal those ugly wounds and focus on creating memorable moments.

What wounds are you holding onto that you need to let go?

Why are you holding on to it? What's the payoff?

If you let it go, what will happen?

We get to choose what we want to
remember and focus on.
Living in the past can be painful. It
can keep you from moving forward.
Learn to look at it and let it go.

When Love is Not Enough

What does one do when love is not enough?

Do you continue to give in or give up?

Does your heart know when to stop and when to start again?

Will a kiss melt the ice that crept over you in the night?

What does one do when love is not enough?

Do you run and hide?

Or pretend that all is right in your world?

Do you break down and cry or scream in the night?

What do you do when you've given your all and nothing seems to satisfy?

What do you do when love is not enough?

I sat in the loneliness of night;

I searched for you in every face I saw;

I cried until my heart felt the hurt, and then, I created space.

I created time.

I created a vision of life without you.

I soon began to smile,

I soon began to laugh,

I soon found myself,

and then, I realized loving myself is enough.

On Saying Good—Bye

If only I could hold you right
here in my arms for a while,
I'd make up for all the lost
time.
I'd kiss and caress you, tell you
how much I've missed you, and leave
the past behind.

We only have this moment to share our
hopes and dreams.
Why waste time in living in the past or
hoping for things that could never be.
I've missed you terribly, my love, my friend.
I wanted to be with you until the very end.

The moments have flown by much too quickly.
It's time to go our separate ways.
May God keep you in His Grace and joy be yours today.

Reflections

There was a time when there was no me without you,
A time when the sun rose as you smiled and my day started when I heard your sweet voice.
Night ended only when I was in your arms.

Now, there is me without you.
But, there is still me with love.
Still me with hopes and dreams.
Still me with tomorrow.
And in tomorrow, I see love.

I feel the love of friends and family.
Smiles from strangers not yet known.
Joy in Mother Nature.
Grace from God above.

Today, while there is no me with you,
There is me and God and that is enough.
With God, I am enough.
With God, I am loved.
God and I together are one.

There are Angels all around us in
the form of friends, loved ones
and strangers.
We need only look for them.

God Sent me
an Angel
Today

God sent me an Angel today;
The Angel came my way.
The Angel held me up and made me strong when I had lost my way.

God sent me an Angel today;
She came in the form of a friend.
Little did I know she would appear and help me mend.

God sent me an Angel today;
Her arrival was not announced,
But God gave her strict instructions to guide and lead me out.

God sent me an Angel today;
Her name I did not know.
The good deeds she brought to me are too numerous to be told.

God sent me an Angel today,
I truly know not why.
But, without her, I know
I surely would have died.

Thanks to my Angel and all the joy she has brought.
Thanks to my Angel for leading me out.
Thanks to my God for the Angel
He sent to me today.

It is often difficult to wait for God's will to show up in our lives,
But if we remain faithful,
All things will work together for our good.

A New Beginning

Today feels like an end without a beginning.
I can't make out the logic; it doesn't feel quite right.
It doesn't feel right because my heart is not right.
My heart is hurting.

We knew love.
I knew what it was like to look upon your face and see that connection only you and I could make.
I long to feel your arms around me and know the security of caring seeping from your eyes.
I think about the years of sharing and intermingling our lives.
I knew then we were in love.

Now, the love is no more.

The nights are lonely.

The phone doesn't ring.

The dreams have vanished.

I stand at the end of the road and look for the new beginning.

I know it's coming.

What do you need to let go of so you can move on in life? What can you do to let it go? If it's time to move on, how will you achieve that goal?

Chapter Four

INSPIRATION

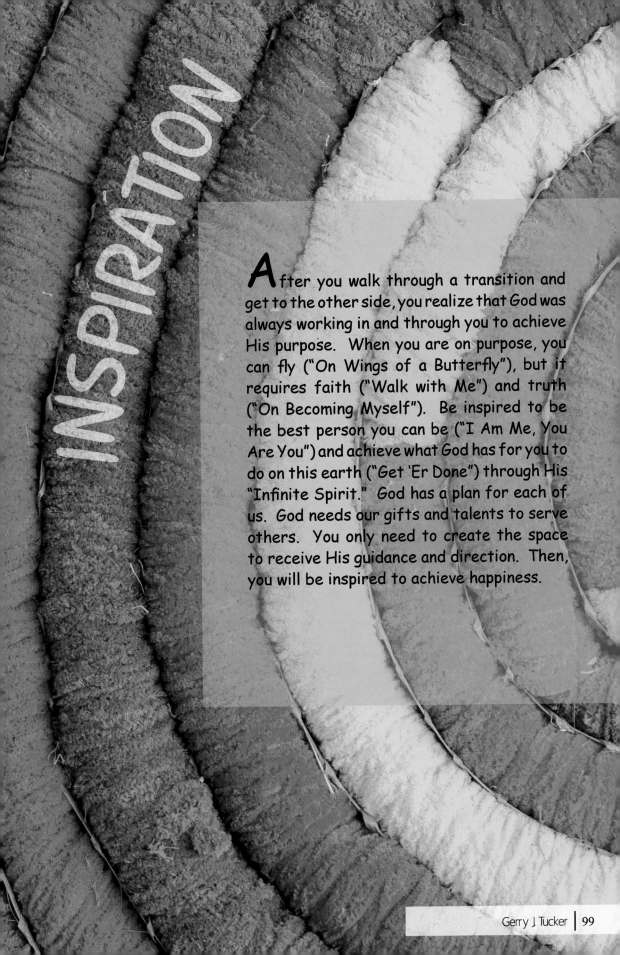

INSPIRATION

After you walk through a transition and get to the other side, you realize that God was always working in and through you to achieve His purpose. When you are on purpose, you can fly ("On Wings of a Butterfly"), but it requires faith ("Walk with Me") and truth ("On Becoming Myself"). Be inspired to be the best person you can be ("I Am Me, You Are You") and achieve what God has for you to do on this earth ("Get 'Er Done") through His "Infinite Spirit." God has a plan for each of us. God needs our gifts and talents to serve others. You only need to create the space to receive His guidance and direction. Then, you will be inspired to achieve happiness.

Achieving Purpose
through Passion

As I lay down tonight, I recognize that I have no passion, no excitement for life. I truly believe that God has a plan for my life, but today God seems silent. I know that God is not silent. God is in everything and therefore, God cannot be silent. When God seems silent, it is because God wants our full attention. God wants us to turn within and depend upon Him. God wants us to tap into the passion that we were given when God created us.

Passion comes alive when you identify the things which you get excited about. It is the thing you are willing to do for the rest of your life, even if you do not get paid for it. Passion is about how you choose to use your time and energy. Passion is about igniting the soul with excitement and love. Passion is about fulfilling one's mission and purpose in life. When you are one with your passion, life opens up to accommodate your desires and you are able to fulfill your life's purpose.

Each of us contributes to the universe in a special way and our challenge is to identify our specific, unique contribution. God needs you to follow your passion and find your purpose. When each individual in the universe is "on purpose," God's plan is carried out.

Passion and purpose are not found easily. It is through tough times and challenges that we find out just how strong we really are and what we value in life. Challenges may mean change; it's not always easy to change our behavior or beliefs. However, change we must. God needs us to change our lives and live according to His will, not ours. It's a constant battle to discover, "what does God want me to do?" rather than, "what do I want to do?" God gives you the desires of your heart, but that doesn't always mean it comes in the form you anticipate. Let God guide you to fulfill your purpose in life. Listen to the still quiet voice within that is calling you to a higher purpose, a higher mission. You will then feel the passion of living a purpose- filled life.

On Wings of a Butterfly

Sometimes we may feel as if we're in a cocoon, fighting our way out of something. It may feel as if we are trapped and cannot get free. Like a butterfly in the early stages of growth, we need to take time to let God form our future and align us with the pattern of our life, a life that God has designed for us.

If a butterfly attempts to rush the gestation period, it fights against the natural order of birth. In due time, it will become a caterpillar, live the life of a caterpillar, and, when the time is right, become a beautiful butterfly.

So, too, it is with your life. God has designed a natural progression for your life. If you attempt to move too fast or pass stages of development, you will miss the order of life. God will put roadblocks in your path to slow you down, create situations to teach you lessons, or put people in your path to guide you to where God wants you to be.

May you grow in God's time and spread your wings, flying about doing God's will. May you carry someone else with you so that they too might become a beautiful butterfly. After all, it's about what you do for others that counts.

Grow into the person God formed in the beginning. You are a work in progress. When you are ready, you will spread your wings, stand on the brink of happiness, and take flight. God wants you to be happy. Spread your wings like a butterfly and fly.

God is right there where you are;
God hears every word you utter,
Even when it doesn't seem like it.

Have faith and believe that if you ask,
God will answer.

Every person seeks to feel the passion in living a fulfilled and satisfying life. There are some days you're clearly walking in the light and other days you can't make your way through the valley. Life is a process. Where you are at this point in time is only a moment in time, there is more to come.

In finding our passion, we find our purpose. Many of us work to earn a living rather than living our lives' purpose. It is rare that we're able to say, "What would I do if I didn't have to…?" There is always something to do and something holding us to an obligation, commitment, or challenge.

Finding one's purpose is about slowing down so that you have the time to love yourself, explore your feelings and feel God's grace. Empty yourself for the purpose of being fulfilled. Be still and listen to that small quiet voice that is guiding you. Often, we want to go full steam ahead to "find it" or "make it happen now." Patience is not one of our calling cards. In patience, we can find peace.

One must know there is a divine plan, a structure

Finding Purpose
Is a Creative Process

to this universe which includes each person as a critical part of the plan. Whenever I feel lost, it helps to see life as a puzzle. Initially, you don't know where all of the pieces go, but you do know that you have them in your hand and you can put them in place, piece by piece. In doing so, you're bound to piece it all together and see the whole picture.

Take the time to look up in the sky and see how the fog covers the clouds and yet, we know there is something behind every cloud. We can't always see what's ahead, but we know that in time we will see God's plan. When we look at the universe, the plants and nature, the birds and animals, newborn babies and our world, we must know that there is a God and we are a part of God's plan. Man can only do so much, and then, there's God.

When it comes to finding one's purpose, the challenge is to find a God-directed purpose. Whom or what issue are you here to serve? What do you care about in life? What do you value? The answer is internal — part of your DNA. It can be found in things that warm your heart, things you love, things that make your eyes water, and your heart light up. It's what brings you joy and pure delight. It's why God put you here on Earth.

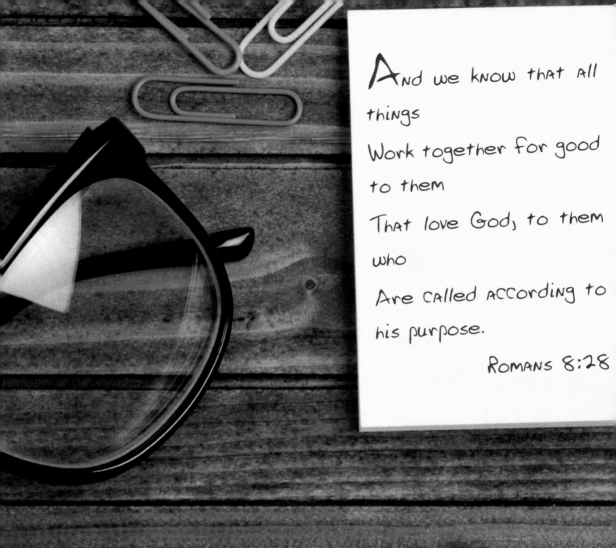

And we know that all things
Work together for good to them
That love God, to them who
Are called according to his purpose.

Romans 8:28

OUR CHAT...

What are your gifts and talents that can be shared with the world?

What can you do that no one else can do?

What is your divine purpose?

The Unseen

I saw the moon light up the dark night.
The same moon that was being seen overseas.
I saw the sun rise this morning
as it moved from the darkness into the bright sky.
I watched the grass grow, but could no longer
see the seed from which it grew.
The torrential rains covered the earth and then,
through a break in the sky, the sun came out.
What man created this plan, this orchestration of nature?
What man gave the command to start the show?
Not a man at all.
But a God that created the universe -
its beginning and its end.
God can start and stop the show in just the blink of an eye.
God created the world and brings it out each day
in His own way.
What man created this plan? It was not man at all,
it was God.

Walk With Me

A bucket list is a wonderful thing. Five years ago I made a travel bucket list with a close friend. Each year we were blessed to check off another trip. One year we decided to return to the Kentucky Derby to celebrate my birthday. Sixteen of my closest friends joined me in a memorable weekend. It was a blessing to share this occasion with them and, boy, did we have fun!

One evening we decided to have dinner at a nearby restaurant. It took some time to get seating for sixteen individuals. Finally, they put us in a private room and we were able to enjoy dinner. There were four sets of my friends some of whom didn't know each other. My college roommate took the lead and asked everyone to introduce themselves and tell about their connection to the birthday girl. We went around the room and some tales were funny, while others were secrets now told. When we got to the last person, she recounted how the year before when we were at the Derby she and her best friend were housed in a less than private room. She shared how my best friend and I had the best suite. In describing their accommodations, she wanted to get our attention to each detail so, she kept saying, "Walk with me." Our response was laughter.

When I think back on it, that's exactly what God was saying to me on that special occasion and it is what God is saying to you. When you walk through the valley, walk with God. When you don't know where to turn, walk with God. When your day goes astray and you don't know what to do, walk with God. When you are at your wit's end, walk with God. God is more than a friend. When you need someone on your side, just learn to walk with God.

Often, it is not what we see, but how we feel. It is not about who you are, but who God is to you.

With God, all things are possible, to him who believes.

Mark 9:23

OUR CHAT...

When was the last time you took a walk with God?

- -

- -

What did you discuss?

- -

- -

Did you get an answer to your question or concern?

- -

- -

- -

On Becoming Myself

I have had heroes and heroines.

I have ruled out the violent, oppressive, and evil roads.

I have used caution and yet, at other times, I have gone
full steam ahead into nothingness.

I spent time in church hoping I would somehow understand
how words written long ago are now directing my life.

I have made choices and decisions in hopes of getting ahead.

I have held my tongue when I would otherwise not have done so.

I have been to many places, met many people, and tried to learn from it all.

I have loved and unloved.

I have played whatever role the years required of me.

And yet, I know not what has become of my "self," my authentic self.

After living life, I have learned that religion is not the same as spirituality.

I can make choices and decisions that make sense only to me,
if I am willing to take risks.

I can accept or reject what someone else says or does.

I don't always have to agree
or give in to someone else.

I can be alone in my thoughts
and not take on someone else's opinion of me.

I can be alone, but not lonely.

When I become myself, I know who I am, good and bad,
what I want and need, and what my life should say about me.

I know to tap into my spirit and breathe,
leaving ego behind and slowing down long enough to hear the voice within.

When I become my authentic self I live from the inside out, rather than from the outside in.

Then, I am free to become myself.

The Past, Today,
and Tomorrow

The past can never be past
   because the past
   is still and will always be
   a part of us.

The part which makes us act and react,
         That which makes us feel and hurt,
         That which makes us what we are today and tomorrow.

You sit upon your throne of happiness to remind me
      that all is not of soul, body, or mind
            But of all that circumscribes our being -
            Yesterday, today, and tomorrow.

I Am Me, You are You

No two birds sing the same song or same tune,
No two flowers grow the same way –
same roots, same leaves, or same colors.
Raindrops fall and then, are drawn up by the sun.
Clouds float overhead and grass grows green under our feet.
Yes, man can manufacture.
But, God does not duplicate.

The sun shines each day and the sky turns colors.
No two suns shine the same.
Animals may resemble each other,
But, none are really the same.
Yes, man can manufacture,
But, God does not duplicate.

God did not make you or me like anyone else.
Even twins are different in some way.
And so our task in life is not the same.
Each to his own to behold;
I am me and you are you.

"Get 'Er Done"

I never thought about having a bucket list until I saw the movie. The bucket list concept became real for me when I experienced the deaths of my mother, father, oldest brother and youngest brother within a few years of each other. By the time it was over, I was exhausted and needed to do something for me.

Little did I realize there was more to do when my mother's small voice echoed in my ear, "get 'er done." I had to ponder what that meant. After much deliberation, I decided she was talking about my bucket list. Years earlier, I had made a bucket list in my journal and had forgotten about it. I needed to start working on it. I pulled it out and went to work.

On the list was Italy. My best friend announced she was going to celebrate her fiftieth birthday in Italy and that was all I needed. Twenty-five of her closest friends made the trip. It was awesome. We stayed at five chateaus on a hillside in Tuscany. Awakening to the dew, fireplace and rolling hills was a sight to behold, not to mention the food! We traveled throughout Italy and the highlight was Rome. In a special audience with the Pope, we were spellbound by the language, in awe of the pomp and circumstance, and overwhelmed with the solemnity of the service.

Next on the list was France. The Eiffel Tower was amazing. We did as much of the Louvre as we could in two days. My daughter stood for an hour watching the painting of the Mona Lisa. I couldn't view the Leaning Tower of Pisa without leaning over to see it. Shopping made the trip complete.

The next thing on my bucket list was to celebrate my sixtieth birthday in a big way! Thanks to my friends, it turned out bigger than ever — a ballroom full of butterflies hanging from the ceiling, friends and family, and tasty food. The night was complete with dancing.

And now that I've checked those things off of my list, it's time to make another bucket list for this chapter of my life. I can still hear my mother saying, "Get her done." I hope you will be as successful with your bucket list — get 'er done.

OUR CHAT...

What's on your bucket list?

How many things have you checked off?

What's the one thing on your list you will regret not doing if you don't get 'er done?

Dream Big Dreams

Υou have three wishes. Wish for anything. Be specific and clear about what you want in your life right now. Don't put limits on your wishes. Don't put limits on God's goodness. Dream Big dreams.

1.

2.

3.

Why are these things important to you?

What do you perceive as obstacles?

What do you need to do to achieve these dreams?

Infinite Spirit

*R*eveal to me the way.

Let me know if there is anything

for me to do right now.

I give thanks to you for guiding me.

I know God is leading me to my greatest good.

Beyond these clouds, sunshine is waiting just for me.

I am worthy of love and good things.

I am centered in truth.

I am aligned with God

in thought, action, feelings, and deeds.

I am vibrant and alive.

I trust that the spirit within will guide me.

I let go and follow my inner voice.

God and I together create and manifest good things

in my life.

To My Daughter...

$\mathcal{D}$ate Unknown

Dearest Geraldine:

    I hope this letter will help to heal your heart by knowing that all your experiences are lessons you learn by living in this world. May our Angels minister to your heart.

    We must ask God for a peaceful solution to our problems and expect an answer. It will come, we will be not know when or where or what will be involved, but we must remain open and aware when God shows us what is to be.

    Try forgiveness. It won't be easy, release the hurt and take a new path and place your future in God's hands. Don't let anything destroy you, your loving nature and trust in other people.

    Remember nothing can hurt you as much as you can hurt yourself, so be good to yourself.

    Don't sweat the Small Stuff. Pray for God to give you a new life, take the darkness away, and fill you with his blessings. He will send you an abundance of his power and you will rejoice in it. God will remove the burden you are carrying, have faith in his Love. Love for you.

Your Mom,

Helen R. Jenkins

Your talent is in your hands, my friend;
Your talent is in your heart.
To grasp the concept of loneliness
And turn it into a picture,
To portray the lovely Christ figure,
Your talent is in your hands.
Some never know their talent, their gift, or their treasures.
Others see them and close their eyes to the truth,
Too fearful to feel its pleasure and acknowledge its roots.
I watched you grow and blossom into springtime,
Pulled back by disappointment and the needs of tomorrow.
I tugged and you pulled the rope away;
you were too far out of reach.
Your talent is in your hands, my friend.
God gave it to only you.
No one strokes the way you stroke a brush,
Nor feels what you feel when you paint.
Your talent is in your hands, my friend –
A gift from God to you.
—Gerry J. Tucker

In Memory

To My Brother

About Spirit Works

SpiritWorks began in 1997 as a metamorphosis from a desire to support individuals in their journey to find their voice, purpose and passion to a monthly newsletter filled with poems, inspiration and biblical principles. For seven years the newsletter was shared with people across the nation who wanted a better way of life and found answers in God's word.

The newsletter, Bedside Chat, was designed to be read before retiring for the night.

Thereby, imprinting in one's mind and soul positive messages. Believing that our thoughts create our world, SpiritWorks empowers individuals to design their future through visualizations, vision boards, affirmations, readings, and believing in the power of faith and prayer.

Through its workshops, SpiritWorks provides a workbook with exercises designed to assist individuals in exploring their purpose and passion with the goal of integrating their human experience with their spiritual nature.

Bedside Chat II will empower individuals to reach higher heights by achieving their goals and dreams. The book explores defining success and stepping into the greatest vision of the person you were created to be in life.

Life is a journey and each chapter is meant to be fully lived so that each of us can achieve our purpose and God's plan for our life. SpiritWorks is here to facilitate your journey.

About the Author...
Gerry J. Tucker

Gerry J. Tucker's mission is to "help bring about a profound change for the better in the lives of other souls; to assist them in re-defining their goals and objectives, evaluating how to make choices for positive change. GOD and I working together can do this."

Whether serving on non-profit boards, managing human resource problems, writing articles and newsletters or conducting workshops, Gerry's passion is working with women to achieve their dreams. As a spiritual, career, and life coach, Gerry does individual, private coaching helping individuals tap into their purpose and passion in order to create a more fulfilling life.

She holds a J.D. degree from the University of Texas at Austin, M.A. degree in Student Personnel Administration from Howard University, and a B.A. degree in English from Fisk University.

For more information, contact:

SpiritWorks

P.O. Box 16311

Austin, TX 78761

www.TheSpiritWorks.net

Made in the USA
Columbia, SC
03 January 2020

86258411R00075